This Journal Belongs To :

Lady Boss
Publishing Co

"THE DIFFICULTIES OF LIFE ARE INTENDED TO MAKE US BETTER, NOT BITTER."

1

Date :   /   /   S M T W T F S

"IF THE GOING IS REAL EASY, BEWARE, YOU MAY BE HEADED DOWN HILL AND DON'T KNOW IT."

2

"ADVERSITY IS A FACT OF LIFE. IT CAN'T BE CONTROLLED. WHAT WE CAN
CONTROL IS HOW WE REACT TO IT."

3

"BREAKDOWNS CAN CREATE BREAKTHROUGHS. THINGS FALL APART SO THINGS
CAN FALL TOGETHER."

4

"IF YOUR KNEES ARE KNOCKING, KNEEL ON THEM."

"IN TIMES OF STORM, THE SHALLOWNESS OF THE ROOT STRUCTURE IS REVEALED."

"NO ONE WOULD EVER HAVE CROSSED THE OCEAN IF HE COULD HAVE GOTTEN
OFF THE SHIP IN A STORM."

Date :   /   /   S M T W T F S

"A BEND IN THE ROAD IS NOT THE END OF THE ROAD... UNLESS YOU FAIL TO MAKE THE TURN."

9

"THE ONLY WAY TO START IS TO START."

"ACCOMPLISHMENT IS EASIEST WHEN WE WORK THE HARDEST, AND IT IS HARDEST WHEN WE WORK THE EASIEST."

Date :   /   /   S M T W T F S

"THE FELLOW WHO DOES THINGS THAT COUNT, DOESN'T USUALLY STOP TO COUNT THEM."

13

"IF COLUMBUS HAD TURNED BACK, NO ONE WOULD HAVE BLAMED HIM. OF COURSE, NO ONE WOULD HAVE REMEMBERED HIM EITHER."

"EDUCATION IS WHAT YOU GET FROM READING THE FINE PRINT. EXPERIENCE IS WHAT YOU GET FROM NOT READING IT."

15

"WHEN IN DOUBT, ASK. WHEN NOT IN DOUBT, ASK."

"A HOUSE IS MADE OF WALLS AND BEAMS; A HOME IS BUILT WITH LOVE AND DREAMS."

19

"LIKE DREAMS, SMALL CREEKS GROW INTO MIGHTY RIVERS."

"HIS LIFE WAS A SORT OF DREAM, AS ARE MOST LIVES WITH THE MAINSPRING
LEFT OUT."

Date :   /   /   S M T W T F S

"IF ALL OF OUR WISHES WERE GRATIFIED, MANY OF OUR DREAMS WOULD BE
DESTROYED."

"YOU CAN MAKE THE DREAM COME TRUE IF YOU WAKE UP AND WORK."

Date : / / S M T W T F S

"A DREAM IS A MICROSCOPE THROUGH WHICH WE LOOK AT THE HIDDEN OCCURRENCES IN OUR SOUL."

28

"TO THOSE WHO CAN DREAM THERE IS NO SUCH PLACE AS FARAWAY."

"YOUR DREAMS WILL COME TRUE... IF YOU CAN SEE IT... IF YOU BELIEVE IN IT... THEN YOU CAN ACHIEVE IT."

31

"THERE IS NO SUCH THING AS ACCIDENTAL FAILURE. ALL FAILURE IS AT LEAST HALF IMPOSED."

"WHEN YOU STAND AT THE EDGE OF THE CLIFF, JUMP TO FLY, NOT TO FALL."

"YOUR FAILURES WON'T HURT YOU UNTIL YOU START BLAMING THEM ON OTHERS."

34

"YOU'RE ON THE ROAD TO SUCCESS WHEN YOU REALIZE THAT FAILURE IS ONLY
A DETOUR."

35

"IT IS A MISTAKE TO SUPPOSE THAT PEOPLE SUCCEED THROUGH SUCCESS; THEY
OFTEN SUCCEED THROUGH FAILURES."

36

"EMPLOYEES TEND TO LIVE UP TO THEIR MANAGERS EXPECTATIONS OF THEM. IF
A MANAGERS EXPECTATIONS ARE HIGH, PRODUCTIVITY IS LIKELY TO BE
EXCELLENT."

Date :   /   /   S   M   T   W   T   F   S

"RARELY DO THE FOLLOWERS EXCEED THE EXPECTATIONS OF THE LEADERS."

38

Date :   /   /   S M T W T F S

"WINNER EXPECTS TO WIN IN ADVANCE. LIFE IS A SELF-FULFILLING PROPHESY."

39

"DON'T MAKE EXCUSES, MAKE GOOD."

Date :　　　/　　　/　　　　S　M　T　W　T　F　S

Date :   /   /   S M T W T F S

Date :   /   /   S M T W T F S

"FAILURE IS THE PATH OF LEAST PERSISTENCE"

44

"JUST BECAUSE YOU'VE LOST DOESN'T NECESSARILY MEAN YOU'VE FAILED."

Date : / /   S M T W T F S

"REMEMBER THAT YOUR FAILURES ARE THE SEEDS OF YOUR MOST GLORIOUS
SUCCESSES. BE SAD IF YOU MUST, BUT DON'T DESPAIR."

49

"SUCCESS IS THE PROPER UTILIZATION OF FAILURE."

"THE GLORY IS NOT IN NEVER FAILING, BUT IN RISING EVERY TIME YOU FALL."

51

"YOU CAN FAIL SO VERY OFTEN. BUT YOU ARE NOT A FAILURE UNTIL YOU GIVE UP."

52

"WE CANNOT DIRECT THE WIND BUT WE CAN ADJUST THE SAILS."

"A WORD OF ENCOURAGEMENT DURING A FAILURE IS WORTH MORE THAN AN
HOUR OF PRAISE AFTER SUCCESS."

Date :   /   /   S M T W T F S

"IF YOU CHASE TWO RABBITS, BOTH WILL ESCAPE."

57

"IF YOU LOOK FOR THE POSITIVE THINGS IN LIFE, YOU WILL FIND THEM."

"IDEAS WON'T WORK UNLESS YOU DO."

"LOOK FOR NO REWARD IN GOODNESS BUT GOODNESS ITSELF."

"ONE WHO MAKES NO MISTAKES NEVER MAKES ANYTHING."

"IT IS NOT WHAT YOU DO THAT MATTERS IT IS WHAT YOU DON'T DO THAT
REALLY MATTERS AT THE END OF THE DAY."

64

"DON'T ASK, DON'T TELL. EVERYTHING LIES IN SILENCE."

"YESTERDAY IS HISTORY. TOMMORROW IS A MYSTERY. AND TODAY? TODAY IS A GIFT THAT'S WHY THEY CALL IT THE PRESENT."

66

"THE ONLY ONE THING I CAN CHANGE IS MYSELF, BUT SOMETIMES THAT MAKES
ALL OF THE DIFFERENCE."

"WHY WORRY ABOUT TOMORROW, WHEN TODAY IS ALL WE HAVE?"

"WHAT YOU SEE DEPENDS ON WHAT YOU'RE LOOKING FOR."

"THE ONLY WAY TO SEE A RAINBOW IS TO LOOK THROUGH THE RAIN."

"WISE ARE THEY WHO HAVE LEARNED THESE TRUTHS: TROUBLE IS TEMPORARY.
TIME IS A TONIC. TRIBULATION IS A TEST TUBE."

71

Date : / / S M T W T F S

"FORGIVENESS IS THE KEY TO HAPPINESS"

"IT IS EASIER TO ASK FORGIVENESS THAN PERMISSION."

Date :   /   /   S M T W T F S

Date :   /   /   S M T W T F S

"BREAK A BAD HABIT -- DROP IT"

75

"PRACTICE IN TIME BECOMES SECOND NATURE."

"PASSION IS THE TRIGGER OF SUCCESS."

Date :   /   /   S M T W T F S

"LIFE ISN'T ABOUT FINDING YOURSELF, IT'S ABOUT CREATING YOURSELF!"

78

"AS THE REST OF THE WORLD IS WALKING OUT THE DOOR, YOUR BEST FRIEND'S
ARE THE ONES WALKING IN."

"A GREAT FORTUNE IN THE HANDS OF A FOOL IS A GREAT MISFORTUNE."

80

"THE WISE MAN SAYS IT CANNOT BE DONE, BUT THE FOOL GOES AND DOES IT."

"WISDOM IS TO THE SOUL WHAT HEALTH IS TO THE BODY."

"NO ONE BECOMES PERFECT, BUT SOME BECOME GREAT."

"SUCCESS COMES IN CANS, FAILURE IN CAN'TS."

Date :   /   /   S M T W T F S

"IF YOU GET UP ONE TIME MORE THAN YOU FALL, YOU WILL MAKE IT
THROUGH"

Date :   /   /   S   M   T   W   T   F   S

Date : / / S M T W T F S

"A GOOD TEACHER IS LIKE A CANDLE - IT CONSUMES ITSELF TO LIGHT THE WAY FOR OTHERS."

91

"EVERYTHING IN THIS LIFE TAKES LONGER THAN YOU THINK EXCEPT LIFE
ITSELF."

93

"THE INFINITE IS IN THE FINITE OF EVERY INSTANT."

"IF AT FIRST YOU DON'T SUCCEED, DO IT LIKE YOUR MOTHER TOLD YOU."

96

"MAY YOUR JOYS BE AS DEEP AS THE OCEAN, YOUR SORROWS AS LIGHT AS ITS FOAM."

97

"THE END OF LIFE IS LIFE. LIFE IS ACTION, THE USE OF ONE'S POWERS AND TO
USE THEM TO THEIR HEIGHT IS OUR JOY OF DUTY."

Date :   /   /   S M T W T F S

"LIFE SHOULD BE MEASURED BY HOW MANY MOMENTS TAKE YOUR BREATH
AWAY, INSTEAD OF HOW MANY BREATHS YOU TAKE."

99

"AN EXECUTIVE IS SOMEONE WHO TALKS WITH VISITORS SO THE OTHER
EMPLOYEES CAN GET THEIR WORK DONE."

100

"IF YOU ONLY LOOK AT WHAT IS, YOU MIGHT NEVER ATTAIN WHAT COULD BE."

"IT IS WISE TO KEEP IN MIND THAT NO SUCCESS OR FAILURE IS NECESSARILY
FINAL."

Date :   /   /   S M T W T F S

"START VIEWING THE POSSIBLE AS PROBABLE. YOU'LL BE SURPRISED AT WHAT YOU CAN ACCOMPLISH."

"YOU NEVER KNOW WHAT YOU CAN DO UNTIL YOU TRY."

Date : / / S M T W T F S

"NINETY PERCENT OF THE THINGS WE TEND TO WORRY ABOUT WE HAVE NO CONTROL OVER, SO WHY WORRY ABOUT THEM?"

108

"PERPETUAL WORRY WILL GET YOU TO ONE PLACE AHEAD OF TIME -- THE CEMETERY."

"BE BOTH THE GARDENER AND THE ROSE."

"BE ENTHUSIASTIC AS A LEADER. YOU CAN'T LIGHT A FIRE WITH A WET MATCH!"

111

"ENTHUSIASM IS THE SPIRIT OF GOD WORKING WITH YOU."

"IF YOU'VE ENJOYED A LITTLE AND ENDURED A LOT, YOU'VE REALLY DONE
PRETTY WELL."

113

Date :   /   /   S M T W T F S

"EACH TIME WE FACE OUR FEAR, WE GAIN STRENGTH, COURAGE, AND CONFIDENCE IN THE DOING."

Date : / / S M T W T F S

Date : / /   S M T W T F S

"EVERY DAY MAY NOT BE GOOD, BUT THERE'S SOMETHING GOOD IN EVERY DAY."

116

"REGARDLESS OF WEATHER, THE MOON SHINES THE SAME; IT IS THE DRIFTING
CLOUDS THAT MAKE IT SEEM DIFFERENT ON DIFFERENT NIGHTS."

Date :   /   /   S M T W T F S

"IF YOU CAN'T APPRECIATE WHAT YOU HAVE GOT THEN GET WHAT YOU APPRECIATE."

118

"THERE ARE ALWAYS TWO CHOICES. TWO PATHS TO TAKE. ONE IS EASY. AND ITS
ONLY REWARD IS THAT IT'S EASY."

Made in the USA
Monee, IL
12 December 2020